C000163228

the little book of the soul
true stories that could change your life

ian lawton

Rational Spirituality Press

First published in 2007 by Rational Spirituality Press.
Second Edition 2008.
Third Edition 2010.

All enquiries to be directed to www.rspress.org.

Copyright © Ian Lawton 2007, 2008, 2010. All rights reserved.

The rights of Ian Lawton to be identified as the Author of the Work
have been asserted by him in accordance with the Copyright,
Designs and Patents Act 1988.

No part of this book may be used or reproduced in any manner
whatsoever (excluding brief quotations embodied in critical articles
and reviews), nor by way of trade or otherwise be lent, resold, hired
out, or otherwise circulated in any form of binding or cover other
than that in which it is published, without the publisher's prior
written consent.

A CIP catalogue record for this title is available from the British
Library.

ISBN 978-0-9549176-2-3

Cover design by Ian Lawton.
Cover image by Jason Waskey (www.jasonwaskey.com).
Author photograph by James Franklin (www.jamesfranklin.com).

Printed and bound by Henry Ling Limited, Dorchester, England.

Contents

This aim of this little book isn't merely to preach to the converted. It's equally if not more aimed at those who have no fixed views about religion or spirituality, and probably don't even have much time to think about such things.

So whether you're young or old, rich or poor, believer or non-believer, this little book is for you.

It's so confusing, isn't it? Why are we all here? What is life for? And who is best placed to tell us?

We've got religion on one side, telling us that we'll survive death and maybe get judged and maybe go to heaven or hell. It gives some people a lot of hope. But others just see how different preachers try to tell us what to do, based on what various prophets may or may not have said thousands of years ago; and how religion tends to divide rather than unite, providing the excuse for countless wars and conflicts. Perhaps we just feel that enough is enough.

Now, we've also got science on the other side, telling us it's all a load of nonsense, and that when we die, we die. They are intelligent people, and their arguments sound so sensible. And anyway, isn't this rational approach just what we need to stop all the killing and bloodshed?

But what about those of us who feel a deep unease when scientists tell us that the physical world around us is all there is? Even more important, is this just because we are so stupid that we need to believe in something more? Or is it because our intuition is literally crying out that they're wrong?

If so, where does this leave the huge numbers of us who strongly suspect there is something more, but are rational and logical and want to see proper evidence and argument? Up until now religion and spirituality have always relied on faith and belief, leaving science to occupy the rational, intellectual high ground.

But is there now reliable, modern evidence that makes it possible to turn all this on its head – and combine the words rational and spirituality in a sensible, meaningful way? And can we for the first time develop a spiritual way of thinking that is properly grounded in evidence, not faith?

The Crying Baby

George Rodonaia had a difficult childhood in Soviet Russia. His parents were murdered when he was very young, and he was adopted by a family from Georgia who showered him with love and made sure he received a first-class education. But then they both died of cancer, within three years of each other, and at the tender age of twelve he was left alone in their home to fend for himself.

George realized he would have to work hard, and he applied himself to his studies with vigor. His big break came when an essay of his was published in the University of Moscow newspaper. It caught the eye of the president, who liked it so much he invited him to attend, even though he was only fourteen. He soon developed into a gifted medical research scientist.

In 1974, at the age of eighteen, he was invited to study at Yale. He was delighted at this recognition of his talents, and at the opportunities it would open up. But the KGB had other ideas. He was researching the way certain chemicals acted on the human brain, and they found this useful for interrogations. If they could not keep him, they did not want the US to have him either.

Over the next two years they put various obstacles in his way but, when he got married and had a child, it finally appeared they would let him leave. Then on the day of his departure, as he stood on the pavement in Tbilisi waiting for a taxi to the airport, he was mown down by a car and pronounced dead at the scene. Bystanders confirmed that, having already sent George flying, the driver had even reversed back to run over him again.

His body lay in a morgue for three days. But as the autopsy began his eyelids flickered, and he was rushed to surgery. Naturally his family and friends were amazed and overjoyed at his survival. But that was only the beginning of a much stranger journey for them all.

As a man of science, George had never had any time for religion: 'I was very much a typical young research scientist and a pretty skeptical one, too. I was not religious at all. I was an atheist. I had basically accepted the materialistic perspective of the hard sciences that everything can and should be reduced to a material cause. There was no room for spirituality for me at all; out of the question, totally out of the question.'

So those close to him were bewildered when, three days into his lengthy recovery, he began to describe what had happened to him while he was 'dead'. He claimed that he had been surrounded by a bright, white light that radiated a sense of peace and joy, and that his whole life had flashed in front of him in an instant of pure understanding. He even claimed that he had been able to travel back to any period in history, and experience it exactly as if he was there, just by thinking about it. Had the trauma he suffered driven him mad?

These doubts mounted when George claimed that he had also been able to travel anywhere he liked while 'out of body'. In particular he was drawn to the newborn daughter of a neighbor. She remained in the hospital in which his body lay because she would not stop crying, and doctors had been unable to diagnose the problem. But much to his surprise he found that he was able to communicate with her telepathically, even though the surrounding adults remained blissfully unaware of his presence. What is more, he was somehow able to scan her body and establish that her hip had been broken at birth.

Incredibly, as soon as George was able to pass on this information, the doctors x-rayed the baby and found that she did indeed have a fractured hip. But how could he have made such an accurate diagnosis while his physical body was lying in a mortuary cabinet? And, even more worryingly for any skeptic, if *this* part of his story was true, what about all the rest of it?

So profound was his experience that, once fully recovered, George threw himself into spiritual study and became ordained as a church minister. He moved to the US in 1989, and in 1996 founded the first international congress on spiritual enlightenment hosted by the United Nations in New York.

Sadly a massive heart attack ended his life prematurely in 2004. But not before he had been able to share his story freely, and to inspire thousands of people through talks and radio broadcasts.

Hotel California

In 1991 doctors told Pam Reynolds, a 35-year-old musician from Atlanta, Georgia, that she had very little time to live: 'They gave me virtually no chance of survival. I will never forget the terrible sadness that permeated the air as my husband drove to our attorney's office for the filing of my last will and testament. Somehow, we would have to tell our three small children that, soon, Mommy would make the journey to heaven, leaving them with the few, short memories their tender years could afford them.'

Pam's problem was that a blood vessel at the base of her brain had ballooned into an aneurysm, and death was the most likely result whether her doctors operated or not. Only one man just might be able to save her.

In Phoenix, Arizona, Dr Robert Spetzler had pioneered a procedure called 'standstill'. Pam's body temperature would be reduced until her heart stopped, then the operating table would be lifted at one end so the blood could drain from her head. He would have about half an hour to fix the problem before her brain would suffer permanent damage from lack of oxygen.

Much to everyone's relief the operation was a complete success. But there was more. Not long after she came round she reported that she had left her body during surgery. She said she had entered a tunnel and then emerged into an intense, bright light, where she was greeted by her beloved grandmother and other deceased family members. Apparently they projected an incredible, 'sparkly' energy into her, and part of her wanted to go into the light with them. But without words they conveyed that if she did she would be changed, and unable to return. So, with young children to raise, and despite some reluctance, she agreed to go back down the tunnel. Her body, still lying on the operating table, felt cold and heavy as she was propelled back in.

Was all this merely her imagination? It seems unlikely, because there is yet more to Pam's story. She also reported on a number of things that were happening in the operating theatre at the time. She said that when she had first floated out of her body she had seen herself lying on the operating table below: 'It was the most aware that I think that I have ever been in my entire life... It was brighter and more focused and clearer than normal vision.'

One detail she remembered was one of the doctors discussing the fact that her arteries were too small. And they subsequently confirmed that they had had trouble inserting the tubes into her inner thighs that would hook up to the bypass machine to cool her blood.

But does this prove anything? We know that she had small speaker-plugs fitted into her ears at the beginning of the operation, to emit regular pulses to check on her brainstem reaction. Yet skeptics suggest that she would still have been able to hear through these, especially if her anesthetic levels were low at the beginning and end of the operation.

They may be right in this. But there is one other element of Pam's recall that cannot be explained away so simply, because it involves sight rather than hearing. She described how, when she first floated out of her body, she also saw Dr Spetzler handling the saw used to open her skull. She said it was shaped like an 'electric toothbrush', with a 'groove in the top', and even commented on the other blades housed in what looked like a 'socket wrench case' by the side.

Again the medical staff were subsequently able to confirm that her detailed description was indeed accurate, even though they were astonished that it came from someone with no medical training. Nor, they said, could she have seen the instrument at the beginning of the operation, because it would have been surgically sealed and hidden away.

Let us be clear that at this point in the operation Pam was fully unconscious, and her anesthetic levels should have been high, even if she would only be clinically dead a little later. Even more crucially, her eyelids had been greased and taped shut right at the start. So how could she 'see' so accurately without the normal use of her eyes?

Pam too has shared her experience widely, especially via her music. She knows that it was not her time to leave – in particular because of the song she heard playing as she returned to her body, which the cleanup team later confirmed had been playing at the end of the operation. It was 'Hotel California' by the Eagles. Indeed she found it particularly ironic that the lyric was 'you can check out any time you like, but you can never leave'.

'Near-death' experiences like these have massive implications. Of course skeptics might suggest that George's and Pam's reports of the 'light' resulted from a mixture of chemicals playing tricks on the brain and vivid imagination. But their memories were lucid and detailed, and are consistent with thousands of similar cases – as well as with other, completely different types of experience that we've yet to discuss.

More crucially still, dismissing them as mere hallucinations doesn't even attempt to account for the verifiable and obscure details that people like this have brought back from their experiences. And as we'll see there are many similar cases in other areas of research where information obtained by unusual means proves not only accurate, but also highly unlikely to have come from pure guesswork or coincidence – because in no sense is it 'obvious'.

The other 'normal' explanation for such impressive cases would have to be deliberate fraud, with the motive of gaining attention and even fame. But is this really likely to apply to a young man like George, who already had a scientific reputation to protect and foster? Or to Pam, who'd surely have little desire to trick people having just survived against all the odds?

What's more, those who come forward often risk ridicule and worse from skeptics. But speak out they do, because they know their reports of other realms are important.

Nor can these experiences be dismissed out of hand as mere hearsay or anecdote. As with most of the other reports we'll look at later, they have been thoroughly recorded and investigated by professionals – that is, fully qualified doctors, psychologists or psychiatrists.

So what do such near-death experiences tell us? They surely suggest strongly that we have a consciousness that survives intact without the physical brain and body. We might even go as far as to call it a soul.

This provides us with our first key proposition:

the soul survives independent of the physical body

But does a soul have just one life on earth, or many?

The GI Joe Dolls

From the earliest age James Leininger of Lafayette, Louisiana had been fascinated with aircraft. He spent hours playing with toy planes, and always pointed and yelled when he saw a real aircraft in the sky.

His parents Bruce and Andrea, a well-educated and grounded couple, were both satisfied that this was just typical childhood behavior – even when James became obsessed with crashing his planes into the living room table that served as his landing strip. But in the spring of 2000, as he approached his second birthday, vivid nightmares began. He would regularly thrash around in his sleep, especially kicking out with his legs up in the air. And it was the words he uttered while writhing that really shook his parents: 'Airplane crash, on fire, little man can't get out.'

They began to fear that his obsession might not be so harmless after all. Why on earth did he keep replaying the actions of a pilot desperately trying to kick out his cockpit window? It was at this point that Andrea's mother, having read a book about similar cases, suggested that these might be memories of a past life. Andrea contacted the author, Carol Bowman, and followed her suggestion that she and Bruce should take the nightmares seriously and discuss them with James.

This did reduce their regularity. But as a result James also started to come up with startling details, usually when being comforted after a nightmare. Over that summer and into the autumn he revealed that the pilot of the plane was also called James; that he had been shot down by the Japanese; that he had flown Corsairs; and that one of his fellow pilots went by the name of Jack Larsen. He also mysteriously mentioned the single word *Natoma*.

Bruce remained dubious about any sort of spiritual explanation, but his curiosity simply would not allow him to ignore the level of detail James was reporting. He knew that neither he nor any other member of their family had any particular interest in aircraft or the war. Nor did he feel that the information could have come from such a young child, who could not even read at this point, watching documentaries without anyone else being aware of it. So, still with the primary intention of somehow proving that there was a perfectly rational explanation for James' memories, he began to research them.

His first port of call was to search for the word *Natoma* on the internet. This quickly established that an aircraft carrier called the USS *Natoma Bay* had been stationed in the Pacific during the latter part of World War II and, among other things, had taken part in the notorious battle for the Japanese island of Iwo Jima early in 1945. Coincidentally his book club catalogue included one all about this battle, so he ordered it, even though at this point he still felt the whole thing was pure coincidence.

But not long afterwards he was really shell-shocked for the first time. One day he was flicking through the book when James came over to sit on his lap, and it happened to be open at a map. Immediately James pointed to the island of Chichi Jima to the north of Iwo Jima and said, 'Daddy, that is where my plane was shot down.'

His interest now well and truly piqued, Bruce continued his internet research and came across a 'Natoma Bay Association', by which means he was able to contact a radioman who had been involved in the Iwo Jima conflict. And although he reported that their squadron had flown only Avengers and Wildcats, not Corsairs, he did confirm that a Jack Larsen had been one of the pilots. This was starting to look like more than just coincidence.

For the next eighteen months Bruce searched military records trying to find out more details about Larsen, but in vain. Indeed he was close to giving up when he attended a reunion of the Natoma Bay Association in the autumn of 2002. Without disclosing his real interest, he was able to establish that Larsen was not dead as he had assumed, but alive and living in Arkansas. Even more revealing, he found out that while a total of twenty-one men had been lost from the *Natoma Bay* during the campaign in the Pacific, only one pilot had been lost at Chichi Jima – and coincidentally his name was Lt *James* M Huston Jr. Aged only twenty-one, he had volunteered to fly that one last mission on 3 March 1945 before he was due to return to the US.

Bruce immediately arranged to visit Larsen in Arkansas, and he confirmed he had been Huston's wingman that day. But neither he nor any other members of the squadron had actually seen what happened to Huston's plane in the heat of battle.

Nevertheless, something else now slotted into place for the increasingly stunned Bruce. His son had always signed his drawings of aircraft 'James 3'. Was this his way of recognizing that his former personality had been James Huston *Junior*, and his father in turn James Huston *Senior*?

At this point the investigation switched to tracking down any surviving members of the deceased's family, and at the beginning of 2003 Bruce made contact with Huston's elderly sister, Anne Barron, in California. Without telling her his true interest they became friendly, and she kindly sent him a number of packages of photos of her long-departed brother.

By this time the only major statement that James had made that did not ring true was his insistence that his former personality had flown Corsairs. Bruce knew that Huston had been flying a Wildcat on that fateful day, and this gave him some sort of faint hope that James' memories might still turn out to be just coincidental. That was until he examined the photographs – because in amongst them was a clear shot of

Huston standing proudly next to a Corsair.

Bruce subsequently confirmed from military records that, before he was posted to the *Natoma Bay*, Huston had been part of an elite special squadron of only twenty pilots, the 'Devil's Disciples', who test-flew Corsairs for carrier use. At this point he finally submitted to what his wife and others had long accepted – that his son James really was the reincarnation of a pilot who had died nearly sixty years before.

But even this was not all, because James made a number of other detailed and obscure statements that turned out to be true. For example, he insisted that Corsairs often suffered with tire punctures, which was confirmed by an aircraft museum. He also said that his former personality's plane had been shot in the engine, which set it on fire before it hit the sea. And eventually Bruce made contact with several members of a bomber squadron that had also been attacking Chichi Jima that day, who all confirmed that they had seen the engine on Huston's plane explode into flame.

As if his detailed recall of names, places and other obscure information were not enough, perhaps the most impressive part of James' recall related to three 'GI Joe' dolls that he called Leon, Walter and Billie. Again military records confirmed that three of the pilots from Huston's squadron who had been killed in other *Natoma Bay* engagements were Lt *Leon* S Conner, Ensign *Walter* J Devlin and Ensign *Billie* R Peeler.

In fact when James was asked why he named the dolls that way he replied, 'Because they greeted me when I went to heaven.' The records also showed that all three had died before Huston.

In an entirely fitting conclusion James is now, once again, in possession of two of his former personality's most treasured belongings, forwarded on by the military after Huston's death and in turn by his sister Anne when she heard the rest of the story: a bust of George Washington, and a model of a Corsair aircraft.

The 1200 Rupees

Madhya Pradesh is a huge, central state in India. It was here that Swarnlata Mishra was born in 1948 – and she was only three years old when she began to reveal amazing details of another life.

On this occasion her father – an inspector of schools – had decided to take her on a trip from their home city of Panna in the north of the state to the central city of Jabalpur, some 170 miles to the south. On their return they were less than a third of the way home when, on the outskirts of the city of Katni, Swarnlata asked the driver to turn down a road towards 'my house'. Shortly afterwards, when they had stopped for a meal in Katni, she again insisted that they would obtain much better food in *her* house nearby.

Of course this puzzled her father, but it was not until some time later that he discovered she was continuing to talk about her previous life in Katni to her brothers and sisters. She said her name had been Biya Pathak.

A number of years passed, during which time

Swarnlata and her family moved some forty miles west to the district of Chhatarpur so that her father could take up a new post. Every now and then she would refer to her past life, but it was not until she was ten years old that he started to take her more seriously.

The breakthrough came when a local professor, having heard a vague rumor about Swarnlata's claims, invited her and her father to dinner. During the meal Swarnlata learned that the professor's wife originally came from Katni, and asked to meet her. Swarnlata's recognition of an old friend of Biya's was instant. And the lady herself was stunned when Swarnlata reminded her of how, in her former life, they had had difficulty in finding a toilet at a wedding in the village of Tilora.

Could a child's vivid imagination alone really come up with such detailed information? Unlikely. Although this time it is not of a historical nature, once again it is not only verifiable but also highly obscure. And certainly the *extent* of information provided by Swarnlata seems to make guesswork statistically impossible, as we are about to see.

For the first time her father now documented the

key statements she had made to date, including that Biya had had two sons, and that her family had owned a motor car – a rarity in this part of India even by the 1950s. She especially recalled a number of details about her former home. Apparently it was white on the outside, with black front doors fitted with iron bars for security. Inside there were four decoratively plastered rooms, while others were less well finished, and the front of the house had stone floor slabs. Behind it lay a girls' school, while a railway line and lime furnaces were also nearby.

Katni is well known as one of the largest railway junctions in India, and also for its lime deposits, so the last two statements might be regarded as easy guesses if Swarnlata were making it all up. But what about the other less obvious details?

Not long after the incident at the professor's house the leading Indian paranormal researcher, Hemendra Banerjee, learned of the case, and he spent two days with Swarnlata and her family in their home in Chhatarpur. He was so impressed that he made up his mind to go to Katni to try to locate her former family. But he knew that Pathak was an extremely common name in the region, so he would only have her statements about her former home to guide him.

Nonetheless in time he was able to find a house that matched the external description, in the right location near to a school, railway and lime furnaces. And the family who owned the house was well known in the Katni-Jabalpur area for their extensive business interests, and were indeed called Pathak. So far so good. But in his wildest dreams Banerjee could not have expected to find that they did indeed have a deceased daughter called Biya. After her marriage she had moved to Maihar, a town some forty miles to the north, where she and her husband had raised two sons. But unfortunately she had died in 1939 from heart disease.

This alone ought to be enough to convince most skeptics. But in fact it was only the beginning of an even more extraordinary case.

In that same summer of 1959 several members of Biya's family decided to visit Chhatarpur to test Swarnlata out. First her eldest brother arrived unannounced at the Mishra family home, but Swarnlata quickly recognized him and called him by the nickname Biya had used, 'Babu'. Then, in conjunction with Swarnlata's father, Biya's widowed husband and one of her sons arranged a meeting in which they were anonymously present amongst nine other local men. Not only did Swarnlata identify them both, but she did so despite Biya's son trying to throw her off the scent for a full twenty-four hours. He insisted that he was someone else, and that a friend he had brought along was Biya's other son. But on both counts Swarnlata stuck to her guns, quite correctly.

Not long afterwards Swarnlata traveled to Katni to visit her former home for the first time. Here she correctly identified a number of people without any leading, and even, again, with a certain amount of deliberate *mis*leading. These included Biya's other three brothers and various other relations; a Pathak family servant; the family cowherd – refusing to be put off by claims that she was wrong because he was dead; and a former family friend and his wife – commenting on his spectacles, which he had not worn when Biya was alive. She also asked about a neem tree in the compound and a parapet at the back of the house, both of which had been there in Biya's time but were now missing.

Further visits to Katni and Maihar followed in

which more people were recognized and statements verified, up to a total of nearly fifty in all. But perhaps the most compelling piece of evidence came from Swarnlata confiding to her former husband that he had taken 1200 rupees from Biya's money box. This was something of an embarrassment that, he confirmed, had been known only to himself and his former wife.

Faced with such overwhelming evidence, it was not long before all parties fully accepted the reality that Swarnlata was Biya reincarnate. Indeed she continued to visit her former family regularly, and their close bonds were re-established. What amazed onlookers was the way that, in the company of her former brothers, she would adopt the attitude of an older sister. And they in turn seemed to accept this as perfectly reasonable – despite the fact that in this life she was their junior by some forty years.

So what do skeptics have to say about apparent past-life memories like these? One normal explanation offered for many cases is that the children involved were combining vivid imagination with information learned normally by overhearing conversations, or from television and radio programs and so on – albeit that their parents remained unaware of, or had forgotten about, these possible influences.

This might seem to work if the families were reasonably close to each other and the murder or death of the 'previous' person was locally notorious. But that certainly wasn't true of the two cases above, in which the children also came up with detailed information that only a handful of people, or even only one other individual, knew about. Nor do skeptics offer any convincing explanation as to why so many children identify with these lives as their own, if they've merely overheard other people talking about them.

What other normal explanations are there? On the face of it, in this area of research it's rather more likely that the children's parents might have deliberately and fraudulently 'coached' them for potential financial reward – especially if the previous family was somewhat wealthier. But this would give the latter every reason to be suspicious and uncooperative – and was almost certainly why the Pathak's initially gave Swarnlata such a hard time. Not only that, but it's clear that in some cases the child remembers a less well-off former life. While in others the current family actively discourages contact with the former family for a long time – especially when they've already been bombarded with comments about their child's 'other mother or father', and are already scared of having to compete for their child's affections.

And, again, we're not just dealing with anecdotes. Most of these children's cases have been investigated by professionals – in particular the team set up by Dr Ian Stevenson, the former head of psychiatry at the University of Virginia, who dedicated his life to this research. They've developed detailed protocols to check for normal transmission of information, and fraud, and since the early 1960s have collated what are now over three thousand cases from all over the world.

Skeptics have questioned some aspects of these protocols, and indeed not only Stevenson's impartiality but that of some of his assistants as well. They've also managed to pick holes in a couple of his cases, and to argue that they should have been recognized as fraudulent. All of this isn't without a certain justification. But to then suggest that the motive for fraud was widespread in his cases, and confidently announce that every single one can be explained by normal means, is going way too far, as detailed analysis shows.

Above all they deliberately ignore cases like those of James and Swarnlata. Not only did these two come up with incredibly obscure information, but their current families weren't particularly poor, and no credible motive for fraud has been shown. So the selective and simplistic dismissals of skeptics just will not do.

But even if we accept some sort of paranormal or spiritual explanation, do these cases necessarily indicate that we have many lives? What if, for example, these children were somehow tapping into some sort of 'universal memory bank'? This seems unlikely, because in most cases their recollections aren't just impassive but produce intense emotions, sometimes pleasurable and sometimes painful, such as James' nightmares. Often, too, they display the strong behavioral traits of the past personality.

Alternatively, could they have been possessed by the disgruntled spirit of the former personality? This would better account for the depth of emotions and unusual behavioral traits. And the fact that the memories tend to fade between the ages of five and nine would arguably correspond to the suggestion that children tend to be more susceptible to possession. But a number of these children briefly mention how they 'hung around' after their death, until they decided to pick some new parents and be born again. This seems to indicate a certain individual continuity from one life to the next.

So it would appear that the best explanation for these cases is that the children are recalling their own individual lives, not anyone else's.

Intriguingly there's equally strong evidence of past lives from another area of research, even though it's often written off as being subjective and unreliable – even sometimes by those who accept the idea of reincarnation. And that's the regression of adults into their past lives, whether by hypnosis or other means.

Most professional psychologists and psychiatrists have a largely scientific training, which tends even now to encourage skepticism about any kind of spiritual dimension. Yet from the middle of the last century an increasing number of such professionals around the globe found that occasionally patients would appear to regress into past lives without prompting. And those brave enough to 'think outside the box' became increasingly convinced that these experiences couldn't just be dismissed. After all, they wouldn't dismiss memories arising from normal regression into childhood, which uses exactly the same technique.

In fact those who actively experimented with past-life therapy found that the results could be incredible. Serious problems that might have resisted years of conventional therapy were sometimes permanently alleviated within only a few sessions. It even seemed that the therapy worked whether or not the participants believed in reincarnation. But the pioneering therapists found themselves sufficiently convinced that they risked their professional reputations by going into print on the subject.

Of course no sensible person would suggest that all past-life memories retrieved by regression are entirely historically accurate. It's perfectly possible for imagination and normally acquired information – whether consciously remembered or not – to combine to create a fascinating and apparently authentic story that doesn't represent a past life at all.

But we've seen that the crucial factor in near-death and children's past-life cases is the recall of detailed and obscure facts that can be subsequently verified. So are there any similarly impressive regression cases?

The story of Australian psychologist Peter Ramster is broadly typical of the pattern described above. In the early 1970s he set up a hypnotherapy practice in Sydney and, despite initial skepticism, became increasingly intrigued by the fragments of his patients' past lives that kept emerging. And he too discovered that these could deliver impressive therapeutic results.

For most therapists this is enough, and they don't feel the need to question the authenticity or otherwise of the experience. But Ramster's insatiable curiosity wouldn't allow him to leave it at that. Instead he decided to experiment with his subjects, in a concentrated attempt to elicit detailed factual information that could be *checked.*

Luckily for posterity, film-making was his favorite hobby. So after a decade of diligent research he was in a position to put his own film crew together, and to take several of his best subjects halfway across the world – to Europe, the setting for the past lives in question. He wanted to see if their detailed recall under hypnosis in Australia matched the facts on the ground.

So, how did they get on?

The Chateau

Amelie de Cheville was the daughter of a wealthy French merchant. They owned a chateau to the northwest of the market town of Flers in Normandy. She grew up alongside her brother Philippe, their every whim attended to by servants, watching with amazement and envy as the beautifully dressed guests arrived for an endless procession of lavish balls. Often these were held by the lake in the grounds of the estate, and minstrels played on as the guests danced long into the night.

But the carefree days of youth could not last forever. Before long she found herself marrying an army officer, and leaving the family home to move to a house on the Rue St George in Paris. She was still comfortably off, with servants of her own, but life was not quite as lavish as it had been with her father. She had two children, Edouarde and Marianne.

As time went on, life became increasingly difficult. The pressure for revolution was building as the gulf between rich and poor widened. Amelie decided to send her children, by now in their mid-teens, to the chateau for their safety. She rarely left the security of her home to venture into the streets of Paris, and when she did she found the streets filthy and overwhelmed by rats.

Then came the fateful day when she was dragged from her house by the mob and thrown into a small, dark cell. Nor was it long before she found herself being forced into a cart. Her hair had been cut short at the back, and she knew what was to come, but first she had to face the crowd on the journey to the square and their hatred left her numb with fear.

She watched as the victims ahead of her met their fate. So great was the bloodlust of the crowd that as soon as one head had fallen they were ready for the next. Every available vantage point was taken, every window and balcony, like some great sporting occasion. The heads were trophies to be stuck on spikes, while the bodies were flung over a wall and left to rot. The streets were literally rivers of blood.

Finally Amelie's turn came. She stumbled up the steps to the guillotine – confused, petrified, jostled and pulled from all sides. Her hands were tied behind her back, and as she was pushed down into position her throat struck the block so hard she nearly choked. Then, staring into the basket, with everything covered in a thick blanket of glistening blood, she heard the final 'swoosh'.

Little did she know that 200 years later she would be back in France, searching for traces of that life.

This was the most detailed of a number of lives that Cynthia Henderson described to Ramster while in trance in Australia, over the course of a number of sessions. It was enough to convince him to take her to France to see if they could find her former home. But it was a big risk, because none of them had even been there before, at least not in *this* life. However they would be aided by a young French Catholic with little sympathy for reincarnation called Antoine le Breton, who would act as the independent witness.

Starting from the bustling marketplace in Flers they followed the route she had described in trance: 'You go past the church for a while, and then you come to a road, a big road that goes between Rouen and St Michel. Go right there for about an hour [by coach], and then it starts to go up after you leave Flers, the road goes over the top of a hill. You can look down mainly on the left side, you can see woods, trees and fields... Then you turn left down to the chateau.'

Coming out of the town past the church and finding the main road north was no great problem, and before long they came to a long incline. At the top there was a spectacular view over a wooded valley on the left, and at the bottom a turning to the left, all just as Cynthia had described.

The smaller road wound around for a while and then, disaster! A new estate had been built, and the roads had changed completely. They could not go in the direction she wanted, so was this to be the end?

Fortunately after asking for directions they were able to pick up the original road on the other side of the estate, and before long she pointed excitedly to a long wall running alongside the road. She was convinced it belonged to the chateau, and that the entrance lay just ahead. As they drove into what was now a public park and slowly made their way up the tree-lined driveway, Cynthia's tension mounted: 'Oh God! I can't look... Oh God, there it is... It's a *tower*!' Previously it had been a tantalizing dream, but now it was a reality, and the emotion was too much. Cynthia began to sob deeply. She at least felt she had come home.

The chateau was a derelict ruin now after suffering bomb damage during the war, but it was not difficult to imagine its former splendor. Two stories high and crafted from cut sandstone blocks; the large porch with huge doors and long windows on each side; the imposing tower at the rear that she and her brother had been forbidden to climb; the lake nearby. All was exactly as she had described it in trance.

Once she had had time to get over the initial shock, they walked around and she soon found everything flooding back to her: 'I feel fantastic here. I feel as if I belong. It's incredible. I recognize everywhere... I have all these images of the coaches and the clothes and the people, the servants and the parties and everything, the whole bit... It's only just now that the impact has hit me, how real those people were, and this was my life! It's all so real to me. It's sort of like a big tunnel being opened up and my whole memory being brought back.'

The team then took her to Paris to see if they

could locate her house there. This time she could not lead them from the outskirts because the environment had changed beyond recognition, but when they arrived at the Rue St George she knew where to look. Unfortunately the building at the site of her former home was completely different. And given her unpleasant memories of this latter part of her life, which were in such stark contrast to those of the chateau, the team agreed not to linger.

Nevertheless they had rather more success in tracing a regular holiday destination she had described as being within a few miles of the picturesque Mont St Michel, on the coast some fifty miles to the west of Flers. This was a large country house that she said had been owned by a friend of Amelie's father.

As the team left the car park at Mont St Michel they were once again relying on the clarity of Cynthia's recall. And this time she had said little about the journey in trance, so they were instead relying on her recognizing the route consciously as they went along. But they need not have worried, because the country roads had not changed too much and she retraced her steps as if it had been only yesterday. She directed them to take a number of turns, without making a single mistake. Then she told them they were approaching a stream, and that their goal was coming up on the right just around a bend – which it was. Again emotion got the better of her and she burst into tears.

Cynthia had described the house itself back in Australia, and the details were borne out when they pulled into the courtyard of a u-shaped mansion, with a central archway through which coaches would once have passed. The only difference was that a well lay in the centre of the courtyard rather than the fountain she had described, but even this could have been the one feature to have changed significantly in the intervening centuries.

As the team walked around Cynthia again felt her surroundings coming to life. She was particularly captivated by the chapel in the grounds of the house, which she had also described previously. Apart from many other details that could perhaps be put down to intelligent guesswork, she had reported that it had a hexagonal stone font on the left, dark wooden pews and, even more obscure, diamond-shaped blue-grey tiles on the floor. And, when the team obtained permission to enter the chapel, yet again all these details proved to be accurate.

This was the initially skeptical le Breton's reaction: 'It is difficult to work it out. It is a fascinating and intriguing experiment. It has reached the limit of credibility. It's absolutely different, I can't understand it. There is something spiritual at the heart of it.'

Remember, too, that all of these events were documented on film by Ramster and his team. In fact they had already investigated another case that was equally if not more impressive in England, to which we will now turn.

The Buried Flagstone

When Gwen McDonald first arrived in Ramster's office she had only come to provide moral support for a friend, who wanted to see if she could experience a past life under hypnosis. Gwen herself was a down-to-earth, middle-aged woman who had no belief in reincarnation at this time, and no desire to be regressed, so when Ramster said he could just as easily work with both of them to see how well they reacted she was initially reluctant.

Nevertheless after some persuasion she agreed, and how grateful we should be that she did because she turned out to be one of his finest subjects. She regressed easily and, albeit with some further reluctance that Ramster had to overcome, agreed to return to help with his ongoing research.

Initially he uncovered ten different past lives with her, which took place in various parts of the world, with the earliest as far back as prehistoric times. But for research purposes he decided that the most promising was a life in eighteenth-century England, a country that again Gwen had never visited in this life – indeed she had never even held a passport.

In trance she initially revealed that her name in this life was Rose Duncan, and that she lived with her father Adam and stepmother Bessie in a small dwelling called 'Rose Cottage', which was part of a larger estate. Although she did not say where this was, it is obvious to anyone just reading Ramster's written transcripts that when she became Rose she talked with a broad Somerset brogue.

The full details of this life then emerged over the course of a number of subsequent sessions. She was born in 1765, and had a happy and relatively uneventful childhood – although she later found out that at birth she had been taken away from her real mother, whose maiden name was Lethbridge, who was married to a Lord Somerville, and with whom her father had had an affair. He went away for long periods so she was mainly left with Bessie, of whom she was very fond, and Dobbs, Bessie's grandfather, who kept her entertained with many local tales and legends.

The highlight of her week was when she crossed

fields and a stream to visit the nearest village to buy provisions, where she could look in the shops and meet local people.

She knew that the master of 'the big 'ouse' was called James Mackenzie, and that he owned various ships that traded around the globe. But he had taken the estate over from a Lord Panmure of Forth, a friend of her father's who was very kind to her when she was young. So she was less fond of Mackenzie, and even less of his annoying son Nicholas. Apparently he chased her for amusement when she was a girl, and for entirely different reasons as she developed into a young woman.

But her greatest pleasure was reserved for when she could walk right through the woods and fields and on to the ruins of the abbey at Glastonbury, which she reckoned to be some six miles away. Sadly, it also proved to be her ultimate undoing.

As she approached the age of eighteen her father began to cast about for a suitable husband. Mackenzie, Lord Panmure and her father were all expatriate Scotsmen – indeed it seems the latter had come to Somerset to hide away in the aftermath of the failed Jacobite rebellion of 1745. In any case, when he returned one day he announced that he had found a suitable candidate from the clan McCrae, and that after their marriage she would go to live in Scotland for good.

Rose was thrown into confusion. The poor girl did not want to leave the home and people she loved, and was not at all sure she was ready to be married, especially not to a complete stranger. Worse still, the McRae's were relatives of the Mackenzies – who by this time Rose had come to hate with a passion.

Desperately confused and scared she ran for miles until she reached the abbey, her favorite place when she needed time to think, but as night started to close in it was too late to try to make her way home. Gradually the temperature dropped and the cold became more intense, so she took refuge in one of the ruined buildings and huddled up in a corner to fight off the cold as best she could.

Her parents had no idea where to look until they asked Dobbs, who knew of Rose's love for the abbey, but by the time they found her it was morning and she was already very ill. They took her home on their cart, and Bessie nursed her in bed. But after several weeks she succumbed to pneumonia and died.

Gwen's life as Rose became Ramster's 'lead' case because it was so rich in detail. But before he could commit to taking her and others halfway around the world, he needed to do some preliminary checking of the accuracy or otherwise of Rose's story. He and a colleague devoted hours to poring over old records in the New South Wales Library, and it proved well worth the effort.

He had specifically asked Rose to name the villages in the surrounding area, and the majority of these checked out on modern maps as clustered together in southeast Somerset. Langport, Somerton, Alford, East and West Pennard, West Bradley and Croscombe – which she correctly pronounced 'Crocom' – were all there within about a twelve-mile radius of each other. Better still she mentioned the villages of Hornblawton – again her pronunciation was quite precise – and Stone Chapel, both of which were correct for her time, although the former is now called Hornblotton while the latter no longer exists.

Ramster also managed to unearth a manuscript from this period that recorded all the landed gentry in Somerset, and he was delighted to find the Lethbridges, James Stuart Mackenzie and Hugh Somerville all listed. Meanwhile Rose had also described how Mackenzie had hired the architect James Wyatt to renovate the stairs and banisters in the main house, and how a curse had been placed on the Mackenzies by Coinneach Odhar, the 'Brahan Seer'. And both these aspects of her story checked out too.

These signs were encouraging. Ramster was also satisfied there was no way Gwen was attempting to perpetrate some sort of elaborate fraud by having accessed similarly obscure manuscripts. So he was now ready to depart for England to conduct his own further research before Gwen and the others joined him.

In the library at Taunton he enquired about the word *tallet*, which Rose had used in connection with the roof of their cottage, and found that it meant a loft.

More impressive again was a discovery he made by pure luck. Rose had mentioned that a group of Quakers used to pass through her neighborhood to get to Alford, where they had a small 'meeting house'. When he looked into this further he discovered that, although in modern times there are meeting houses in virtually every town and in many villages, at that point they were rarer. But Alford was not listed in the main Quaker records from that time, and nor did anyone in Alford itself know of such meetings having taken place.

However, during his local research he and some assistants chanced upon a hoard of magazines from the period, and they happily flicked through them out of general interest and to get a feel for life in Somerset at that time. They did not expect to find a brief but clear reference to a meeting of Quakers in Alford. This was starting to be the sort of obscure information that even the most determined hoaxer was unlikely to have uncovered.

As if all this were not enough already, Gwen and the film crew then flew out to meet Ramster in London. After a little rest and acclimatization, Ramster again regressed Gwen to her life as Rose, and afterwards discussed the details consciously in the hope that her memories would now be closer to the surface as they tried to verify them.

This seemed to work because they then traveled to Somerset to meet Basil Cottle, an expert in local history from the University of Bristol who was to act as an independent witness throughout. She was given an unmarked map of Glastonbury and asked to point out any landmarks she recognized, and immediately identified Wearyall Hill, which lies to the southwest and which she had referred to back in Sydney. She also identified Tor Hill to the east, on which stands the famous ruined tower of St Michael's Church. She then pointed out the ruins of the abbey on the map, and for the first time described how two low pyramids had sat in the middle of the ruins, acting as a doorway. A local historian subsequently confirmed that this observation was correct according to medieval records.

Gwen's next stop was to be taken to the abbey itself, although blindfolded so as not to prejudice later attempts at navigation. When she first saw the ruins again she was clearly moved. The major difference, apart from the absence of the two pyramids, was apparently the way in which the site had been cleared of rubble and generally cleaned up for tourists – which in fact she found rather sterile and depressing.

But as she walked around the memories seemed to come flooding back. She lovingly caressed the carved feathers on the pillars of an arched doorway, exactly as she had described Rose doing all those years before. At this point she became quite understandably overwhelmed because, despite the detailed nature of her hypnotic recall, she had never been consciously certain of its validity. Until now when, just like Cynthia, she realized she really had stood in exactly this spot nearly two hundred years previously: 'The memory of this place brings the same old feelings and the feelings of peace. You wouldn't believe the feelings I get inside from seeing this place, you really wouldn't.'

The next task was for Gwen to attempt to find her former home, which the team felt sure had been in Hornblotton. She was blindfolded and taken to the outskirts of Ansford several miles to the east, which they also felt sure was the local village she had walked to once a week. Standing in a field she spotted a line of trees to the west that she thought were familiar, and the search was on.

She took them along a road for a short distance,

but then stopped at a bend in the small village of Clanville. She said that in Rose's day there had been a row of five houses at this point, one of which sold cider. Now there were only two new houses and two old ones, one a mere ruin. But in the other the owner confirmed that his house had been built in 1742 and that a number of its contemporaries had only recently been knocked down. Not only that, but his family had a tradition that one of them had been a cider house – a point subsequently confirmed on an old map.

Gwen now left the road to the north and began to traverse the fields. It was not long before they came to the stream she had said would be there, but it was getting late so they decided to stop for the day. The next morning they returned and she led them along the stream, still heading west. In trance she had described how they would come to a fork, near which was a small waterfall, all of which they encountered after about a mile. In addition, although she had described some stepping stones near the fork that were no longer there, a local man was able to subsequently confirm they had been removed some forty years previously.

At the fork Gwen sensed she was close and sped

off across a field, with the rest of the team struggling to keep up. After about half a mile her mood changed to one of trepidation as she stopped and stared at a building that could just be made out through the trees. When they reached it there were tiles on the roof rather than thatch, and it seemed to be just an old barn attached to a more modern home. But she insisted this was her old house.

Cottle asked Gwen to sketch the back of the house on the spot, and she came up with a rough drawing of a back window and door, and of a lean-to that she referred to as the drying room. When they walked around there was a lean-to, but only one window that looked as if it might have once been a door. Cottle was skeptical, yet Gwen was convinced this was her former home and, facing it again after an interval of several centuries, she broke down in tears for the first time.

Their differences were soon resolved. The team obtained permission to look inside, and the outline of an older window that was now bricked up lay exactly where she had said it would. Meanwhile there, in the roof, was a loft room or tallet.

This, surely, must be the end of Gwen's incredible

story? No. There is one final, and even more amazing, twist. While in Sydney she had described how Rose had been at the abbey one day when she had cut her foot quite badly, and a local farmer called Brown had taken her to his cottage nearby to bandage it up. He was kind, but the forthright Rose was upset that he had been stealing flagstones from the abbey ruins to cover the floor of his home, because on this particular journey she was sharing the cart with one that had unusual markings on it. Ramster asked her to draw these while still in trance and she very roughly sketched a variety of curved lines and spirals.

Of course they had already had incredible success with Gwen, far more than they could possibly have hoped. But Ramster knew that the crowning glory would be if they could locate the farmer's cottage and the flagstone, even though the chances were probably slim at best.

So, on their final day together, they assembled at the abbey and Gwen headed off. On the way they passed the George and Pilgrim Inn, which she had described and accurately drawn for Ramster back in Sydney – with a long bow window on one side, an arch in the middle for coaches, and two triangular, pointed structures on the roof. The only difference was that she had called it 'The Pilgrim's Inn', which was correct for Rose's time.

They pressed on, heading west out of Glastonbury towards Meare. At one point they had to skirt an embankment where a new ring road was being constructed, and of course the majority of the buildings had changed too. Nevertheless she persevered, and they eventually came to a bridge over a stream. Now they needed to locate what Rose had described as the second in a row of five thatched cottages that lay nearby.

Gwen left the road and walked along the stream for a short while, before pointing to a dilapidated building on the other side that on closer inspection turned out to be a chicken shed. The farmer, Dennis Simmonds, confirmed that it had been a row of five thatched cottages, which had deteriorated so much that the end ones had been pulled down. What was left had a corrugated iron roof, while the windows were open holes, but it looked as though the basis of the original, second cottage was still there.

The next problem was that for decades the floor had been covered in droppings. Simmonds kindly agreed to clean it overnight, and was himself amazed to find dark blue flagstones that clearly matched others still remaining at the abbey. But what of the one with the markings? Gwen pointed to one that seemed to have faint patterns on it, and anticipation mounted as they washed it off and brushed it with talcum powder so that the markings stood out.

Although faint, there were some definite similarities with the ones Gwen had drawn. And even if one were to take the view that this was purely a coincidence given their relatively random nature, the mere fact that she knew there were flagstones from the abbey buried underneath all the detritus is surely impressive enough.

The main argument used by skeptics when discussing past-life regression is similar to that for children's past-life cases. They suggest that subjects are constructing narratives from normally acquired information that they themselves have forgotten they learned, which is formally called 'cryptomnesia'. In other words they rarely suggest deliberate fraud, but they do suggest delusion.

In this context another fascinating case study is provided by the 'Bloxham Tapes', which were the subject of a bestselling book and BBC television documentary in the 1970s. The star was a Welsh housewife dubbed 'Jane Evans', who recalled impressive historical details of a number of different lives. In the most striking she was the wife of a children's tutor in Roman Britain; a persecuted Jewess in twelfth-century York; and a maidservant to a wealthy financier in fifteenth-century France.

The investigators took great care to establish what the sources of normally acquired information might have been, and to show that most details Jane recalled for each life could only be found in various obscure reference works. However they overlooked one major source, and that was historically based fiction. Indeed skeptics were able to show that her Roman life was closely based on a historical novel, despite her use of strange accents and strong apparent emotions while in trance. So it's clear that we need to tread carefully.

Nevertheless it turns out that Jane's French life can't be explained in the same way, despite skeptics' claims. In fact it's arguably one of the strongest cases on record because, for example, she recalled the financier having been given a 'golden apple encrusted with jewels'. The existence of this piece was subsequently traced by a local historian to contemporary court records, written of course in medieval French, which hadn't been accessed for centuries. Such obscure information surely wouldn't appear in any work of fact or fiction, nor in any other normal source.

The same is, of course, true of the most obscure facts in Ramster's cases. But these remain so poorly recognized outside his native Australia that few skeptics have even heard of them.

Yet even if normal explanations fail in these strong cases, could the alternative paranormal explanations that we rejected for children's past lives apply this time round? Again some sort of universal memory seems unlikely to be able to account for the depth of emotion felt by Cynthia and Gwen when they were reunited with their former surroundings. And while on the face of it possession again appears to be a more feasible solution, neither woman showed any of the unusual behavioral traits normally associated with this. Again, therefore, the recall of individual past lives seems the most likely explanation for these two cases – and perhaps for many others as well.

We've spent some considerable time on the stories of James, Swarnlata, Cynthia and Gwen. But this is because our second key proposition, which stems from them, has significant and far-reaching implications:

souls have many lives, not just one

So far so good. But is there any evidence that can help us to really understand what happens after we die – that is in the time between lives? And does this evidence show a continuity across many lives that reinforces our conclusion concerning individual soul memories?

The Hall of Records

What follows is Gwen's account of what happened *after* Rose's death, again elicited by Ramster using hypnosis, although his questions are omitted here.

'I died in bed, and old [Dr] Andrews was sitting by my bed with my father and Bessie. Then my father, he walked out the door. And Bessie, she be crying [these seem to be the last remnants of Rose's Somerset brogue before her soul-self takes over].

'Then I saw a lady, I knew her last time [I died]. She was with a man in a long robe, and he put out his hand and I took it and I went with him. I began to feel very light, no weight, nothing to hold me down, everything was light, like floating but not floating. There was no pain, and I was very aware, so much more aware of feelings and senses, and thoughts, almost as if you didn't have to speak. It was like being made of air. Free, free, so free.

'Before I left I remember standing beside the bed and looking down at the body. I'd wasted away, and I felt free, so free. I was just standing there looking at myself and I wondered why Bessie was crying. Then I realized I was dead and the life was no more, and I couldn't go back, it was over. I could see Bessie crying. I knew she couldn't see me, nor could she hear me. I would have liked to talk to her, but I was dead and could remain there no more.

'I was taken to a place and was told to rest, which I did. I don't really know for how long, but I was being pulled back because Bessie was feeling so sad missing me, and it was holding me back. I came down to see her again and I tried to tell her to let me go, not to hold me back, because it hurts. After a time she finally did.

'I was taken to a place where I met a man who looked like an Egyptian. From the place where I was told to rest we walked along a grassy path. Everywhere was grass and there was water. It was in many ways similar to earth, but you could put your feet into the water and take them out again without having to dry them, as they didn't get wet! He said it was because we were in spirit.

'We walked to the Hall of Records and that was where I met the Egyptian. He was so kind, he showed me all I had done, and things I should have done but didn't do. The place was like a library and it's full of records. It was a big place, a very big place. It had a long corridor with a sort of gold light everywhere inside. He showed me my life, but I could see it in my mind, not on paper, all the things I'd done, things I needed to do and didn't do.

'The thing I needed to do was to be more conscious of other people. I was selfish, I only thought about myself and where I lived, my home, and not the poor people in the village and the poor children. I should have helped, but I didn't. His voice is almost music, and there is a light that shines around him. When he looks at you his eyes seem to read what you are thinking, he seems to know.

'I was told that in the Hall of Records there is a file on every living soul that ever incarnated, and each time we have to see what fools we've been, what mistakes we've made. We have two paths to choose. If you take the wrong path it's all against you. If you take the right path it's all for you, and it's balanced out in the Hall of Records. It's all there, every page, almost every thought and every deed is there, every book, every spoken word you can find. It's gold inside, lit up with a gold light, pure light. Everything in there is knowledge, and the keeper, the Egyptian in this plane, looks after and controls the records.

'We can't touch the higher levels. We can go to the lower levels to try and help, but we can't touch the higher levels until we've been lifted up there as our right. He can go to the higher levels. He can come and go as he pleases, he is close to the master, but you know he's there. You can feel he [the master] is there, but I don't think he's like we are, I think he's different somehow. I don't think he's like us, I think he's pure spirit. It's just a feeling you have that he's so far out of your reach. You wish you could touch him, but you can't, he is far above us.

'We reincarnate to learn, to learn knowledge, understanding and compassion. Those who do not learn must come again and again and again... That is why we must come back, until our souls are pure enough to stay up there on that level. Because our thoughts are what makes us, and what colors our soul.

'When we leave the Hall of Records the Egyptian bows, puts his hands together and smiles. When the door shuts, you know what you have to do, it's all in your mind without him saying a lot. It's in your mind, it's there.

'After going over my life we left the library and were back on the grass. We paddled in the water and, as I said, didn't need to dry ourselves. There were boats on the water, all green grass and trees greener than anywhere. The flowers were all alive, no dead flowers. Around the lake on the other side there were more trees, flowers, and birds, pretty birds, and oh, such beautiful music! We sat and talked under the trees and rested. It was a beautiful place. The only time I became worried was when someone thought of me and I was pulled back, and it's sad.

'Finally a man came, he said I must go back to earth. I didn't want to go back but I had to. He said there were people who needed me and I must help. There were two families who needed me, and I had to choose. I could do what I had to do with both families, but I had to choose, and I must go back. I rested on that plane until it became time to go back to earth.'

Ramster wasn't the only therapist to be amazed when he discovered that some of his subjects could recall lucid details, not only of their past lives, but of their time between lives as well. A number of other 'interlife' pioneers in America and Canada made the same discovery in the mid-1970s. All of a sudden ordinary people like Gwen were delivering profound insights into what happens in what we might refer to as the 'light realms'.

But, unlike past-life recall, this isn't the sort of experience that can be verified. So can it really be regarded as at all reliable? The reason we might answer 'yes' is that these pioneers were all operating independently in what were pre-internet days, and yet the reports from their hundreds of subjects were broadly consistent. These people had no particular religious or spiritual background, but instead came from a broad cross section of Western society. And not only were the books the original pioneers published not widely enough read to have had a significant influence, but most of them had completed their early research before their books even came out.

Before we get carried away we should appreciate that interlife experiences are extremely fluid, which is why it's probably a mistake to attempt to over-categorize them. For example, Gwen talks a great deal about a semi-physical place with grass, trees, flowers and water, and even of a 'Hall of Records' run by someone she calls the 'Egyptian'. Some other subjects have reported seeing similar things, and have even referred to a 'hall' or 'library'. But others tend to perceive both their environment, and any other souls they meet, in more energetic and less physical form. It seems that much of what we experience, at least while we're getting used to being in the light again, depends on the assumptions we bring with us from our earthly lives. Our general level of soul experience may also be relevant.

Nevertheless, despite this fluidity, we can broadly identify five main elements of the interlife experience that are consistent across all the pioneering research. And Gwen's account provides a fine example because she at least touches on most of them.

So what are these elements? And, more to the point, what can they tell us that might help us to better understand how to approach our everyday lives?

1. Transition and Healing

Gwen talks about being met by a man and a woman who are there to guide her after death. And most interlife subjects talk about being met by deceased friends or family, or other spirits of light who help them to make the transition. The same is also true of most near-death subjects, as we saw earlier with Pam.

Gwen also talks about feeling 'light, very aware and free' as she's released from her body, and again most interlife and near-death subjects talk in similar terms. It seems that we have to shed the denser emotions and energies associated with the physical world so that our soul energy gradually becomes lighter. We might refer to this as 'delayering', and it seems that this raising of vibrations is essential to allow us to re-enter the higher frequencies of the light realms.

This process also seems to be closely tied into emotional healing, although the extent that this is required depends on the degree of trauma suffered in the previous life – and death. Gwen seems to need little after her life as Rose, because she's merely told to rest. But other subjects describe incredible 'cleansing showers of energy' that invigorate and lighten them, and wash away many of the stresses and strains of the physical world.

But not all is sweetness and light. The evidence suggests that some souls who are heavily traumatized don't even realize or accept that they're dead. As 'ghosts' they remain tightly focused on and attached to the physical, unable to let go of their deep emotions of fear, anger, jealousy, hatred or revenge, and often feeling they have unfinished business.

It seems that the energy of such spirits is so dense that they remain unaware of, or at least unable to move into, the light. Instead they hang around in what we might refer to as the 'intermediate plane', the nearest to the physical in terms of density of vibrations. And any 'astral travelers' who encounter this realm, whether via projection or meditation or drugs, rightly report that it's extremely unpleasant. Indeed, if there is any such place as 'hell', this is it. But it appears that these spirits are certainly not condemned to live in such torment for eternity.

2. Past-Life Review

We've all heard how our life flashes in front of us when we think we're going to die. And the idea of reviewing the life just lived is again common to not only interlife but also near-death experiences, as we saw earlier with George. It seems that sometimes we have help with this from two possible sources. On the one hand 'spirit guides' – that is, experienced souls who are always on hand to help us. And on the other various 'elders' – even wiser souls who help us to plot a path through our successions of lives.

Like Gwen, subjects often describe these reviews as taking place in a library-type environment, although the books often seem to 'come alive' like a film. Others suggest that they can 'enter' the film to replay various events, or even to role-play them by doing things differently and seeing what happens. And some even report that they can place themselves in the shoes of others, to see exactly what effect their own actions had – which, intriguingly, seems to tie in with the effect of the natural hallucinogen iboga.

Above all, and unlike in most religions, interlife research suggests that the only judgment in this review process comes, if at all, from ourselves. This is because our 'soul perspective' is totally unlike our human outlook, and cannot include self-deception or excuses. All our actions and, even more important, intentions are laid bare – and these are all that matter because, as Gwen says, they're 'what makes us, and what colors our soul'. Some souls find this dramatic change of perspective extremely uncomfortable, of course. So more often than not our spirit guides and elders are there to calm and reassure us, rather than to judge.

3. Soul Group Interaction

Interlife research suggests that all of us have a 'group' of 'soul mates' with whom we work closely over many lives. But the relationships can vary. Sometimes we're lovers, sometimes siblings, sometimes parents or children, sometimes close friends – and sometimes even enemies, just to spice things up. We can also change sex from one life to the next, which is perhaps a better explanation of why some people carry over gender identity issues than the simplistic 'nature versus nurture' debate.

When we reunite with our soul mates on our

return to the light it's always a profoundly moving experience. We finally feel like we're 'really home'. Gwen doesn't recall meeting up with her soul group in that particular session, but she does insist that 'we reincarnate to learn'. And the evidence suggests that the primary aim of all souls is to gather experience in order to learn and grow. So our time with our soul group often involves discussions about lives we've shared, how we reacted to each other, what we handled well and what we could have handled better. And it appears that the ability to replay and role-play events is extremely useful for this learning process.

But what do we really mean by 'learning'? And how does this relate to traditional ideas of 'karma'?

The Guilt That Wouldn't Go

Jenny Saunders first visited the pioneering interlife psychiatrist Joel Whitton at the University of Toronto because of sexual problems. He was known locally as the 'lost cause doctor' because he could cure people when all other therapies had failed.

Over a prolonged and difficult period of conventional regression he managed to establish that she had been cruelly abused by her mother as a child. She therefore avoided sex because any feelings of pleasure brought on by sexual stimulation were immediately replaced by emotional pain and intense anger. This realization should at least have started the healing process, but Jenny's symptoms persisted.

Whitton had also discovered that she was terrified of having a child of her own, and not long before becoming his patient had had an abortion after a rare sexual encounter. Apart from the obvious fact that she might not want to repeat the mistakes of her own mother, he could find nothing else in her current life to explain this fear. So he decided to extend the regression back beyond her childhood, at which point the following two lives unfolded.

As Lucy Bowden she had been the poverty-stricken single mother of a mentally retarded child in London in the late seventeenth century. In those days everyone regarded such children as a mere burden to be disposed of, but Lucy cherished and protected her child with all her might. She rarely left her rented attic room because of her fear that someone, whether well meaning or not, might try to rid her of her 'burden'.

But one day she went to fetch some provisions, and stopped to have a drink with some friends at an inn. Not used to alcohol, time slipped by quickly until she realized she had been gone for some hours, and rushed home. But when she turned the corner into her street her blazing house was surrounded by curious onlookers. Pushing through the crowd, she realized there was nothing she could do to save her child – and her unbearable inner torment was to set up a recurring pattern.

In another life in the mid-nineteenth century Jenny was Angela, a young girl abandoned by her parents and brought up in a Chicago orphanage. At sixteen she left the harsh institution behind to seek a new life in the mid-west, ending up as a barmaid and part-time prostitute in a small town in Colorado. The local doctor fell in love with her and she became pregnant by him.

But, unbeknown to her, the local parson began berating the doctor that his child would be born out of wedlock to a woman of ill repute. Eventually he blackmailed the doctor into agreeing that it should be committed to an institution to preserve its moral sanctity.

So as soon as the child was born the parson, the doctor and two assistants came to collect the baby, wrestling it from the convalescing Angela's startled grasp. Instinctively she reached for a shotgun she always kept under her bed for protection, but in the ensuing struggle the weapon discharged right at the baby and the assistant carrying it, killing both instantly.

Again Angela's shock and remorse was unbearable, but worse was to come. Their curiosity piqued by the sound of a gunshot, and with the parson egging them on to punish the 'murderer', six cowboys entered the room and dragged her off to a cattle shed, from which she never emerged.

After reliving these horrors Jenny wept uncontrollably in Whitton's office – maybe for the first time in her life.

How should we interpret Jenny's experiences? The traditional view of karma, still expressed in many spiritual circles, is that it involves some sort of 'law of action and reaction'. So, if we have problems in our current life, this is often assumed to be a reaction to something we did wrong in a previous one.

But how can this apply in Jenny's case? She was primarily an innocent victim in not only her two past lives when she lost her child each time, but also in her current one in which she was abused as a child. This is clearly a 'repetitive' pattern of sorts, but not one in which she alternated between victim and perpetrator in a cycle of action and reaction.

Many people would nevertheless assume that she must have done something awful in other lives – ones that she didn't recall during her time with Whitton – to deserve such 'punishments'. But then we find that when Whitton regressed Jenny into the interlife, she perceived herself appearing before her elders in chains.

His interpretation was that, just as we've already seen with past-life reviews, she was meting out her own punishment because of her failure to forgive herself for letting her children down in her former lives. So she gave herself another difficult life, although with a rather different pattern, because that was what she felt she deserved.

It therefore seems that any repetitive patterns we set up from life to life will probably be quite complex, as in Jenny's case. And simplistic interpretations, especially if they involve suggestions of action and reaction, are unlikely to be of much use. What we do know is that with Whitton's help Jenny came to realize that she had to forgive herself for her past-life mistakes. And happily, when she left his office for the last time, she was no longer afraid. Indeed she was determined to have a child in this life too.

So it seems that the traditional idea of a karmic law of action and reaction, which determines our fate or even punishment from one life to the next, is entirely unhelpful and misleading.

But what about Gwen's insistence that we reincarnate to learn? We find that this sentiment is echoed time and again by interlife subjects. Indeed it's the most constant theme of all.

Regression evidence suggests that in the first instance all souls have to work on what we might refer to as 'emotional lessons'. That is we need to learn how to shift progressively away from fear-based emotions and attitudes such as impatience, guilt, shame, selfishness, humiliation, jealousy, anger, hatred and revenge towards more love-based ones such as patience, altruism, openness, understanding, forgiveness and acceptance. And in order to experience and understand them properly we need not only to feel them ourselves, but also to feel what it's like to have them directed at us by others.

So, even if they can be quite complex, it appears that we do tend to indulge in repetitive patterns of behavior as we attempt to master our emotions, either within one life or from one life to the next. But it's clear that this shouldn't be regarded as in any sense backward or abnormal. And one of our aims in all of this is to learn to moderate our emotional responses, not only to difficult but also favorable circumstances. Wise advice down the ages, from all over the world, has always been that we shouldn't get too carried away by our successes, nor become crushed by our failures.

What, then, do we make of difficult circumstances, such as severe disability, or emotional and financial deprivation? Clearly *traditional views of these as karmic punishments for past misdeeds are totally misplaced. And even though there can of course be repetitive elements to them, modern evidence suggests that such circumstances are most often chosen by relatively experienced souls who want to speed up their growth. This indicates what we might refer to as a more 'progressive' pattern of behavior.*

It also seems that more experienced souls increasingly choose to take on more 'altruistic lives', which tend to be primarily for other people's benefit and growth rather than their own. This can involve severe disability, but the most obvious example of a purely altruistic life is when a soul volunteers for a short life that'll end in childhood, or even before birth. Although such lives can sometimes be traumatic for the infants themselves, they tend to be far more aimed at challenging parents and other close relatives to learn to cope with the myriad emotions that surround such a tragic loss. And Jenny's two past lives involving young children are, of course, prime examples of this.

We're now in a position to make three more key propositions:

our many lives are not linked by a karmic law of action and reaction

we reincarnate to gather experience so we can grow

the only judgment after death comes from ourselves

4. Next-Life Planning

To continue with the next element of the interlife, while the idea of a past-life review may not be particularly novel, there is nothing in traditional religions to prepare us for the idea that we're involved in planning our own lives. Yet this is what the interlife evidence consistently suggests, and it has huge implications for the way we see ourselves.

But first let's look at the mechanics of this planning process. It seems that at the very least it'll involve an awareness of what sex we'll be, who our parents will be, where they live and what their circumstances are. However many subjects seem to receive a rather fuller preview, often describing it as akin to seeing a film that they can stop, rewind, fast-forward and even enter to fully experience what's going on. We may even be given a preview of several different lives, and be asked to choose which one we think will provide the best environment for our growth.

In Gwen's example she was at least told there were two families who needed her to help them in her next life after Rose – suggesting perhaps a more altruistic flavor – and that she could do what she had to do with either. So presumably she was given some sort of preview of each to allow her to make her choice, although this wasn't discussed in that session.

As usual, our spirit guides and elders are on hand to help with this planning process. We may also spend some time discussing our plans with other members of our soul group who'll be involved in that life, and even agreeing 'triggers' that'll help us to recognize them when we meet.

So what are the implications? If we can see detailed previews of our life, does this mean it's all totally predetermined? Apparently not. It seems that these glimpses merely represent the most probable outcome if we stick to our 'life plan'. The key point is that we still have complete free will to stray from this once in the physical world, because a predetermined experience would provide no opportunity for making decisions for ourselves – which is a major contributor to our growth. This also means that when we face difficult circumstances we would do well to accept responsibility for them. Not only did we choose them, but we did so to allow ourselves to grow. And we won't achieve this by attempting to put the blame on other people, a fickle God, or blind chance.

We can summarize this into two further key propositions:

we are responsible for all aspects of our lives because we plan and choose them

we always have free will to deviate from our life plan

5. Returning

Gwen seems to suggest that she was forced to return to the physical world. However the broader evidence suggests that most of us 'know' *when it's time to continue gathering experiences in the physical, even if we may have some initial reluctance to leave our true home in the light.*

Recent interlife research also suggests that when we return to the physical we leave some soul energy behind to carry on with various activities in the light realms. But we take with us specific emotions we want to continue working with, and even past-life strengths that we may need to help us through difficult patches. It seems that this is achieved by what we might refer to as a 'relayering' process, in which we take on these heavier emotions as if putting on various layers of clothing.

Our soul energy can begin to merge with the unborn child in the womb at any time from conception to birth. This is a gradual and sometimes difficult process, which seems to involve some sort of matching of the individual pattern and frequency of our soul energy to that of the developing brain. But we can also relax by floating out of the body for short periods, not only up until birth but even for some time afterwards.

Of course we all know how much babies sleep, and it seems that this is our way of becoming gradually accustomed to the physical again. In fact babies probably retain a significant memory of their true soul identity and connection to the light realms – which is why they should never be underestimated. However over time this connection gradually fades, for two main reasons. First, if it didn't we'd be constantly pining for the bliss of our true home. And second, if we remembered all about our life plan it would be like taking an exam with all the answers to hand – and we'd learn nothing.

And so begins another cycle on our lengthy round of gathering experience in the physical world. But how long does this reincarnation cycle go on for? And what happens when it's over?

All the evidence suggests that, broadly speaking, we keep coming back for as long as the physical world can offer us new experiences that'll allow us to grow. After that we can still come back sometimes to help others, or we can move on to other less physical planes to continue the process. Either way it seems that, in terms of the soul's overall journey, finishing with the 'earthly round' is only the end of the beginning.

But what of 'God'? Does He, She or It exist? Gwen's reference to 'the master' as an apparently separate being probably reflects a certain simplicity, because the answer is most likely 'yes, but not in the way you might think'. The central element of all mystical and transcendental experiences seems to be a brief glimpse of the 'Oneness' and interconnectedness of everything in the universe. This comes from experienced meditators, and from those who experiment with 'altered states' using hallucinogenic drugs. Most tellingly it's now also backed up by modern science.

So it seems that everything in the universe, both seen and unseen, is part of one interconnected whole or 'Unity' – often referred to simply as 'Source'. Indeed we might go as far as to propose that 'we're all One and all God'.

Because of this, some people suggest that the idea of us being individual souls is just an illusion. But in this book we've painstakingly amassed a great deal of evidence to the contrary. So is there a way of accepting both sides of the evidence – that is, for soul individuality and unity?

The answer is yes. What if soul consciousness is

holographic? This would allow for us being individual aspects of Source, and full holographic representations of it, all at the same time. Remember that the principle of the hologram is that the part contains the whole, and yet is clearly distinguishable from it.

Let's conclude by daring to consider the biggest question of all: why does any of this happen in the first place? Some might think this is far beyond mere mortals and that we should leave well alone. But surely we should at least hazard a guess?

Some people suggest that we only need to recognize that we're part of the One to escape from the illusion of the reincarnation cycle. Yet what would be the point of the whole exercise if that was the case? Others maintain that the whole idea of soul individuality is an illusion, and that when we die our soul energy automatically reunites with Source. Meanwhile the new breed of spiritually oriented, theoretical scientists – or 'quantum mystics' – sometimes seem to struggle to put their theories about unity, interconnectedness, even multiple worlds and so on into a sensible, understandable, overall framework.

But what if the answer is actually dead simple? What if Source's primary aim, in diversifying into all the billions of holographic aspects of itself that operate in the various realms throughout the universe, is to experience all that is and can be? And what if, as individualized aspects of Source who have chosen to reincarnate on this planet, we are merely fulfilling a small part of that objective by gathering a balance of all the experiences available here?

So here are our three, final, key propositions:

we are all One and all God

soul consciousness is holographic, and represents the part and the whole all at the same time

the aim of Source is to experience all that is and can be

A Personal Story

It might be useful to conclude by saying a few words about my own story. If this little book is successfully finding its way to the type of person I hope will find it most stimulating and rewarding, we should share at least some things in common.

I was born in 1959, and brought up on the south coast of England. In common with so many households of my generation ours was at least nominally Christian, although I can't remember religion ever being discussed much. But we had to sit through lessons and sermons at school, and as soon as I started to really think for myself I realized that these left me cold. Without wishing to cause offence, from a purely theoretical perspective Christianity seemed to me to be completely irrational.

So it was that I became convinced that religion was for those who *needed* to believe because they were too feeble to exist without that vital crutch. By contrast, I decided, real power and strength comes from within oneself, not from some external deity. What I didn't know then in my youthful arrogance, and what prominent atheists like Richard Dawkins have still not understood, is that there is far more to this than meets the eye.

After I left school I led a rather uneventful life for a while. Instead of traveling the world in my gap year like my more adventurous friends, I worked for a merchant bank in the City. Then off to UCL to study Economics, badly, before following all the sensible advice and going into accountancy.

This was a great training in many ways, but it wasn't really for me. So, after qualifying, a major career change saw me join the yuppies selling computer software. This was the selfish, money-obsessed 1980s, and I fitted right in. In fact I had been racing bikes for some time, with limited success, but the injuries were piling up and I turned to racing cars. With my loud suits and ties, mullet haircut, racing Porsche and blonde on my arm, I surely was the man. Or so I thought. Spirituality? Pah!

So what happened between then and now? Nothing sudden. Just a gradual intensification of a gut feeling that there was something more – coupled with various coincidences, perhaps better termed synchronicities, that led me away from that world and into this. By the mid-1990s, although I was now working in consultancy rather than sales, I was becoming increasingly sick of the world of commerce. The preoccupation with money and contracts and deals and deadlines and targets and progress and success and...

So one day I just quit.

Admittedly I had a bit of money put away although – surprise, surprise – it turned out to be nowhere near enough. My decision was also made far easier by having no family to support. So what was I going to do?

All I knew was that I had a vague desire to start researching some of the ancient mysteries that a partner had recently introduced me to. And so it began. Having had conspicuously little academic success – at least not in any truly creative, intellectual sense – I had no idea that I'd end up writing. I especially had no idea that that writing would eventually take a spiritual course. But it has. And in particular I've found myself drawn towards developing the kind of evidence-based spirituality that you've read about here.

But if I'm honest this recent leg of my journey has been a real struggle. Not just financially at times, but even more emotionally. Constantly trying to compete with hundreds of other spiritual books, let alone those about cookery and football and celebrities and so on, just to get what you hope is a useful idea in front of people. Trying to maintain integrity in your work when others want you to 'sex it up' or cut it down or generally mangle it to make it more commercial. Constantly being promised support, and that one breakthrough you need, only to have your hopes dashed at the last minute.

But of course I must remember to practice what I preach! So I recognize that all this has helped me personally to grow, and to learn some really important lessons about arrogance, expectations, impatience, blockages and positive thinking. More than this, though, there's one major reason why I've persevered even when I felt completely crushed. It's because I believe the concept of 'Rational Spirituality' – which I've been developing for a number of years now, and which is what this book is all about – is sufficiently powerful and unique that it can really make a difference at a crucial point in our collective learning curve.

Why? For thousands of years we've had morality-based religions of all shapes and sizes, sometimes giving hope and succor, but just as often bringing domination, suppression and even annihilation. Then along came science, and it started to prove that our religions were not quite all they'd been cracked up to be. So the smart intellectual money began to shift entirely in a scientific and materialist direction.

Now at last, thanks to the work of many different pioneers from many fields, we can see the real possibility of bringing science and spirituality back together, as they once were in Classical times. But the full power of *all* the modern research at our disposal should be harnessed – that is the evidence that points not only towards universal but also individual soul consciousness. Hopefully the concept of the holographic soul may have a part to play in this – but only in as much as it modernizes what the most profound spiritual sources from across the ages have always tried to tell us.

Rational Spirituality has its roots firmly planted in the fertile soil of modern evidence and logic. By contrast traditional religions tend to be based on unquestioning reliance on ancient scripture, and modern interpretations of it. The motto 'evidence not faith' is intended to convey this fundamental difference in approach. But that's not to say that faith, or perhaps better trust, doesn't have its place. Total trust in our ability to face and pass the tests we set for ourselves and to consciously create our own reality – with assistance from our higher selves, spirit guides and the universe in general if we're open to it – is fundamental to a Rational Spiritual worldview. Nor does it underestimate the power and majesty of transformative spiritual experiences, or underplay the ultimate spiritual message of universal, unconditional love.

Perhaps most important of all, in contrast to many traditional religions, Rational Spirituality doesn't attempt to provide a definitive moral code. Instead it merely encourages us to take personal responsibility for applying its framework of understanding to our own lives.

It is, surely, an idea whose time has come.

Source References

Anyone interested in examining the evidence in this book in more detail, including further cases, more in depth analysis and full source references, can find all this in *The Big Book of the Soul*.

Meanwhile a simple, short companion volume, *Your Holographic Soul – and how to make it work for you*, provides more details on this concept in particular, as well as self-help advice based on the framework of Rational Spirituality.

THE CRYING BABY

Phyllis Atwater, *Beyond The Light* (Thorsons, 1995), chapter 1, pp. 16-17 and chapter 5, pp. 78–82 (for further analysis concerning the baby girl's broken hip see www.ianlawton.com/nde4.htm).

Phillip Berman, *The Journey Home* (Pocket Books, 1998), chapter 2, pp. 31–7 (reproduced at www.ianlawton.com/nde3.htm).

HOTEL CALIFORNIA

Dr Michael Sabom, *Light and Death* (Zondervan, 1998), chapter 3 and chapter 10, pp. 184–9.

THE GI JOE DOLLS

Wes Milligan, 'The Past Life Memories of James Leininger', *Acadiana Profile Magazine*, December 2004 (reproduced at www.ianlawton.com/cpl3.htm).

Leininger, Bruce and Andrea, *Soul Survivor*, Grand Central Publishing, 2009.

THE 1200 RUPEES

Dr Ian Stevenson, Twenty Cases Suggestive of Reincarnation (University Press of Virginia, 1974), chapter II, pp. 67–91.

THE CHATEAU, BURIED FLAGSTONE AND HALL OF RECORDS

Dr Peter Ramster, *The Search for Lives Past* (Somerset Film & Publishing, 1990), chapter 6, pp. 211–43, chapters 2–3, and chapter 2, pp. 57–61.

See also 'The Reincarnation Experiments' documentary produced by Ramster in 1983 (available via www.ianlawton.com/rsvideos.htm).

THE GUILT THAT WOULDN'T GO

Dr Joel Whitton and Joe Fisher, *Life Between Life* (Warner Books, 1988), chapter 12.

Further Reading

This is a selection of the most important introductory books on each topic, which are mostly by professional psychiatrists and psychologists.

GENERAL

Lawton, Ian, *The Big Book of the Soul* (Rational Spirituality Press, 2008) and *Your Holographic Soul* (Rational Spirituality Press, 2010).

NEAR-DEATH EXPERIENCES

Dr Peter Fenwick, *The Truth in the Light* (Berkley Books, 1997).

Dr Raymond Moody, *Life After Life* (Bantam, 1976).

Dr Kenneth Ring, *Life At Death* (Quill, 1982).

CHILDREN'S PAST-LIFE MEMORIES

Carol Bowman, *Children's Past Lives* (Bantam, 1997).

Dr Ian Stevenson, *Twenty Cases Suggestive of Reincarnation* (University Press of Virginia, 1974) and *Children Who Remember Previous Lives* (University Press of Virginia, 1987).

Dr Jim Tucker, *Life Before Life* (Piatkus, 2006).

PAST-LIFE REGRESSION

Dr Edith Fiore, *You Have Been Here Before* (Ballantine Books, 1979).

Dr Peter Ramster, *The Truth about Reincarnation* (Rigby, 1980) and *The Search for Lives Past* (Somerset Film & Publishing, 1990).

Dr Hans TenDam, *Exploring Reincarnation* (Rider, 2003).

Andy Tomlinson, *Healing the Eternal Soul* (O Books, 2006).

Dr Helen Wambach, *Reliving Past Lives* (Hutchinson, 1979).

Dr Roger Woolger, *Other Lives, Other Selves* (Bantam, 1988).

INTERLIFE REGRESSION

Dolores Cannon, *Between Death and Life* (Ozark Mountain Publishers, 1993).

Dr Shakuntala Modi, *Remarkable Healings* (Hampton Roads, 1997).

Dr Michael Newton, *Journey of Souls* (Llewellyn, 1994) and *Destiny of Souls* (Llewellyn, 2000).

Andy Tomlinson, *Exploring the Eternal Soul* (O Books, 2007).

Dr Helen Wambach, *Life Before Life* (Bantam, 1979).

Dr Joel Whitton and Joe Fisher, *Life Between Life* (Warner Books, 1988).

Note also that there are brief references to the interlife in both Fiore's and Ramster's books listed in the past-life section.

Ian Lawton was born in 1959. In his mid-thirties he became a writer-researcher specializing in ancient history, esoterica and spiritual philosophy. His first two books, *Giza: The Truth* (1999) and *Genesis Unveiled* (2003), have sold over 30,000 copies worldwide.

In *The Book of the Soul* (2004) he developed the idea of Rational Spirituality, also establishing himself as one of the world's leading authorities on the interlife. And in *The Wisdom of the Soul* (2007) he first introduced the idea of the holographic soul. His other books include *The Little Book of the Soul* (2007), *The Big Book of the Soul* (2008, a complete rewrite of the 2004 book), *Your Holographic Soul* (2010), *The Future of the Soul* (2010) and *The History of the Soul* (2010, a revision of the 2003 book). For further information see *www.ianlawton.com*.